D1031894

School Buses

Julie Murray

Abdo
MY COMMUNITY: VEHICLES
Kids

abdopublishing.com

Published by Abdo Kids, a division of ABDO, PO Box 398166, Minneapolis, Minnesota 55439.
Copyright © 2016 by Abdo Consulting Group, Inc. International copyrights reserved in all countries.
No part of this book may be reproduced in any form without written permission from the publisher.

Printed in the United States of America, North Mankato, Minnesota.

102015

012016

 THIS BOOK CONTAINS
RECYCLED MATERIALS

Photo Credits: iStock, Shutterstock, ©legenda p.7, ©Sheri Armstrong p.11 / Shutterstock.com

Production Contributors: Teddy Borth, Jennie Forsberg, Grace Hansen

Design Contributors: Candice Keimig, Dorothy Toth

Library of Congress Control Number: 2015941779

Cataloging-in-Publication Data

Murray, Julie.

 School buses / Julie Murray.

   p. cm. -- (My community: vehicles)

ISBN 978-1-68080-133-0

Includes index.

1. School buses--Juvenile literature. I. Title.

629.222/33--dc23

                    2015941779

Table of Contents

School Bus

Mya is ready for school.

What is she waiting for?

The school bus!

Here comes the school bus!

It is big. It is yellow.

The bus has big wheels.

It has lots of windows.

A safety door is at the back.

It is for an **emergency**.

SCHOOL BUS
EMERGENCY DOOR

STOP

84321

STATE LAW

R-32

The driver stops the bus. The lights **flash**. The stop sign comes out.

The door opens. The kids get on the bus. They sit in the seats.

The bus driver makes sure the kids are safe. She gets them to school on time.

School is done. The kids get back on the bus. They ride the bus home.

Do you ride a bus to school?

Parts of a School Bus

emergency door

stop sign

mirrors

windows

Glossary

emergency
a serious and often
dangerous situation.

flash
a short burst of light that usually
shines over and over again.

Index

abdokids.com

Use this code to log on to abdokids.com and access crafts, games, videos, and more!

Abdo Kids Code:
MSK1330